To Helen,
my friend and
a great inspiration
in the work you do
and the life you
live.
All of my very
best is wished for
you. always.

Fatherless Boys

and

Mothers

On Their Own

1st Edition

by J. W. Doncan

Bloomington, IN Milton Keynes, UK

authorHOUSE

AuthorHouse™
1663 Liberty Drive, Suite 200
Bloomington, IN 47403
www.authorhouse.com
Phone: 1-800-839-8640

AuthorHouse™ UK Ltd.
500 Avebury Boulevard
Central Milton Keynes, MK9 2BE
www.authorhouse.co.uk
Phone: 08001974150

First published by AuthorHouse 6/28/2006

ISBN: 1-4259-1708-9 (sc)

Printed in the United States of America
Bloomington, Indiana

This book is printed on acid-free paper.

This book is dedicated ...

To My Son — Danny

To My Mom — Isaac

Both poised and irrepressible -

I love you beyond words.

With many thanks also ...

To Greg Benton whose technology brillance tremendously
aided this endeavor;

To my friends from whom I continue to learn. I have benefitted
from the generosity of your suggestions:
Gaylen Branon, Yves Labissier, George and Sunrise Bishop;

And to my brunch buddy, mentor, and fellow author,
Joe Franklin.

Introduction

It seems that conformity of actions or behavior are the only alternatives from emasculation for young men. Misogyny, extreme competition, and xenophobia are part of a process of conformity that damages young men's (and women's) individuality and esteem. Societies that throw irrelevant questions to the masses like, "Is he a real man?" and proceed to answer with mass media hyperbole - displays and pundits - cause everyone to suffer. Here in the United States, many fatherless boys begin as a gentle group who act with great individuality, sensitivity, honesty and equanimity — until society's poster children for their gender convinces them that these humane qualities should be replaced by those more becoming of "real men."

Single moms are a growing population who, while giving our best to raise honest, spiritual, thoughtful, and respectful children, watch xenophobes and sometimes other very well meaning individuals attempt to overrule our sons' and daughters' individuality of expression and thought with a more simplistic, less threatening to status quo, and a more recognizable set of proscribed attitudes and responses to loved ones and their environments. This painful, deadening process seizes our children's self-esteem and relegates each to another brick in the wall.

Mothers on our own, in raising our sons, become ultimate "tragic comics," smiling through tears while racing to counter the somnambulistic effects of media and society that pummel the fine minds and hearts of our sons. We mothers work fervently - while attempting to be two parents - to fuel changes that will honor our sons' individualities and humane qualities, and to promote an environment where fatherless sons need not waste energy and talent defensively posturing for a phantom group of "real men."

This is a shout out to fatherless boys and single moms. Change in our society's appreciation for you is just around the corner. And this book is riding the crest of that rising tsunami of new attitudes.

Table of Contents

Nemesis? Vanquish Them.

In Praise of All Our Moms

The Finish Gives Meaning to the Race

Community & Educator Discussions

Give the
Fatherless Boy

★

Some Elbow Room

M en have incredible dreams and fears that can paralyze their
steps — a human condition most fatherless boys are not taught at
home to deny. Fatherless boys are forced to be their own fathers, and at
the same time, applauded for not being their fathers. With the anxiety
that comes from this murky territory, American xenophobes have a field
day. But mothers know from experience who the "real men" are!

I'll Tell You A Story ...

He cherished a piece of the sun
Then swallowed it into his heart
He wrapped a rainbow around his shoulders
And headed into the dark.

He followed the path of his dreams
That led to the stream of his truth
It frolicked and laughed and whispered
Dimensions as wondrous as youth.

The valleys were fertile
The mountains serene
He gazed high then low
Then the path of his dreams ...

Vanished before him
And vanished in back
And the eyes that adored him
Seemed torn from his sight.
A storm began brewing
And shut out the light...

Replacing the sun in his heart
And his sky was now troubled and dark.
And the only remains
Of his beauteous terrain
Was the calm distant song of a voice.
Though it sang it brought pain of his loss.
And he tried to recall whose it was.
He sat in the dark and he tried to see light
But the stars closed their eyes
And how dark was his night.

He wasn't alone.
He had not lost his way.
But the breathtaking brilliance so high where he'd climbed
Temporarily stunned him...
His inner sight – blind!

And below was so distant and chilling and cold.
Fear had grabbed his attention
So great was its hold,

That the truth in his heart
Had refused him of sight
'Till he regained his strength ...

Not to stare at the dark down below
Not to stare in the light in the sky.
But to follow the path of the dreams that he'd had
Before large clouds of fear draped his eyes, stomped his voice
To an almost inaudible far distant noise.

And the faint distant song had been this
"Harmony is integrity's bliss - reminisce!"

His strength and his song, led him blindly along
Inner vision – his gift.
Again blossomed so strong!

The impression indelibly carved
That the path of his dreams had its start,
It's direction and end in his heart.

Bounce

Through it all, no matter what
My son you just keep getting up
And half the battle's won.

The sun just may distort your way.
The night — conceal your path — It might.

Imaginings may bloom and loom
Unwarranted, inside your head from fear.

But when you just keep getting up,
You soar from searing sun to shade.
You dance from darkness into dawn.

And monsters in your mind
Made from your fears
Will fade like shadows 'neath the sun.

So dearest one, my darling son ...

Through it all no matter what
My son you just keep getting up
And half the battle's won.

You Are Not Your Father

You are not your father, son,
You are your own man
Complete with your own words and deeds and ways to understand.

You'll build your own bridges
Which you'll cross and you'll return.
It is your decision if there are bridges that you'll burn.

You'll move mountains you've created
And by knowing, they'll dissolve.
Mysteries that puzzle others may be mysteries you solve

Life is not a bowl of cherries
Life is not a pot of pits
Life is rarely that extreme son,
But it's what you make of it

You are Santa, Easter Bunny, the Tooth Fairy, and Sand Man.
But you could be someone scary,
Like a scary boogey man
It's all how you understand son,
And it's right there in your hands.

God has graced you with such wondrous gifts
Uniquely you will stand,
Journey calmly to your future,
And be loved in every land

You are not your father, son,
You are your own man.

Never Let them Tell You Who You Are

I've known you from suckling babe to twenty-two
And I don't claim to know every aspect of you
So when others make a glaring, foolish claim
And your ego is the focus of their slam
Keep in mind that
They have no idea who you are.

Yes, you're gentle; I have seen you tearful and
You help others, just because you know you can
You're soft spoken — when there is no need to shout
But you've also wailed a rock song — kicked it out
Your quiet manner's not a meter
Pointing to the range of who you are.

And you've cheered — a joyful swimmer — for your team
And you've feared for others so you've taken blame
Some broadcast the worst from no disclosures made
They fill lines because they need a written page
With no proof — but their assumptions
And not even knowing who you are!

A fatherless household is who has brought you up
Yells, cruelty, and force are not your strongest suit
But narrow, panicked, xenophobes — they agitate
When your enlightened actions reach beyond their gait
Their ignorance — proof positive
Of negative capacity for knowing who you are.

Give them a turn at feeling a position of defense
Accuse them of the ghosts they see as inner selves and pent.
Stand back and let them writhe and lash out
'Cause they'll want to fight
Stand back 'cause you'll be targeted

Because they know you're right

And how could you be so astute when they'd self-aggrandized?
And how could you see them beyond the focus of their eyes?
When they have screamed out clearly
Who they want the world to see
Regardless of the monsters that they are —
Will always be.

I do believe that monsters are proactive when they speak
Announcing who they are before you have a chance to think.
And like a bird puffed up with feathers signifying naught
Their statements are deflections to protect their sorry lot.

Identity anxiety's the goal of others bashed
To turn a person on himself with nothing left intact.
But turn the tables and create a comedy
Announce their deficits as joke butts —
Who else would they be?
Who else deserves the ridicule of measurement?
To fall short in an arbitrary steep descent?
Eliminate their phantom of entitlement.

And won't they be surprised — unable to explain
How like the phoenix once succumbed and forced to change
You're now in front and stronger yet from striving up
And you've surpassed them as you snag the victor's cup
Though they have never had to make your lonesome trek
I doubt that they could ever struggle and bounce back.
Though ignorance is not a term used lightly here
Search your accusers. They are filled with this and fear.

Fight back as you have always done with wit and charm
While exercising strategy and growing strong.
And like the game of chess that you have learned so well
Leave them confused as hell ...
And never knowing who you are.

The Universe Whispers Weapons

Little Black boy sprouting up like a weed
The world thinks you won't make it
'Cause you started out so far behind
Your sweet spirit?
Some try to break it.

Some think you will sit in the tears that you cry.
But I know you will paint your days brighter.
You won't aimlessly watch as the years roll by.
Armed with love, you my son are a fighter.

And continue to fight when others forget.
Fight with love, resolve, patience, remembrance
Fight the enemy — fear — who is still out there
Timeless weapons do vanquish its chances.

Don't forget these brave weapons your Mother has given
Your Mother - our great universe
God knows if there's one who has sight of the light,
It is she, always showing you truth.

We'll continue to smile — you and I, 'cause we know
The secrets the Universe told
When others are met by the roadblocks ahead
Take your weapons as friends; be reminded by them.
Be tenacious; be humble; be bold.

The universe whispers weapons!

Our Vigilantly
Independent
Sons

Is there a masculine dream? A feminine dream? Are there masculine
solutions? Feminine solutions? What about fears? Or do we all
carry within us different combinations of these - that societies attempt
to categorize by gender? Many fatherless sons remain true to their own
combinations, regardless of the pressure to conform and the odds against
their success - keeping us open and honest.

Two Generations At Breakfast

Today at breakfast we laughed and haltingly took turns
One after another smiled and added approximately
Two cents – give or take.

Mom tried to stay appropriate
Though through passion this was difficult
We all made it through the meal.

But a simple wreathed offering I tossed
Bared its sharp edges and cut in all directions before
It became dried carbon fueling a volatile airborne volume.

It was heavily consumed
Igniting magnetically - nervous laughter, seething silence
And lastly – an attempt to extinguish the resulting heat
Then it fell with a splash like gasoline.

A quelled attempt at intimacy
An apologetic resignation to hostile and phrenetic silence
The air briefly had been stirred.

Maybe at a later date
This will give way and nurture fragrances and songs
But for today overtures were slapped back
And four people left to resume their distance in the four corners of the
world.

The Lake

Swimming eases my mind
I come here to ease my heart
When the sun turns down its light
And I slide into the cool
I become an intrinsic part
Of God's dark, quiet pool.

No one is here to hear me
If I should cry before I wake
From this bad dream without my love
No one's here but my friend the lake.

And gentle fingers brush my tears
Kiss my eyes, tell them it's okay
To blend with the brine
The salt from mine
To stay for a time.
So I'll stay.

She laughs as I lie on her belly.
Her currents pull me along.
The lily pond leaves
The rustle of reed
The slow ebbing speed
Lulls a sleep over me,
While the wind whines a whispering song

And away I will stay
While I heal, while I mend.
With the sole company of the lake, my friend.

Train

Hard times - no job, no family here anyway
I'm going to ride with this train and be on my way
Anywhere it goes away from here is fine with me
Anyplace but this place is the place I want to be.
And if this train could take me to another land
God, I would go. None would ever see this face again.

No one but God knows ...
       Is there human kindness in some space, or place, or time?

No one but God knows ...
       Where is it that the sun is peaceful, gentle when it shines?

No one but God knows ...
       Where does the wind respectfully blow, calling out my name?

No one but God knows ...
       Where are the stars that beacon brightly with their twinkle game?

No one ...
And everything's all right?
       But God ...
       And everything's all right ...
           God knows
           Everything's all right.

Prehension

I can't hold the world together
       Though my hands are laced in prayer
But I can send out a message, though,
       Of love to everywhere.
I can listen very carefully
       To neighbors when you speak
I can restate what I think you've said
       And ask you to repeat
I can set aside the time it takes
       To discuss issues well
I can ask you to affirm my grasp
       Of what you've had to tell.
And in every way to my avail,
       Yes I can reassure
That lovingly I'll walk with you
       Till you're peaceful and secure.

Perennial Weather

My compliment's a couplement
Within, there's joy and merriment
Bewildering, this heaven-sent
That ebbs and flows, but never went
Which never lent a moment's time
In anger spent.

Past Remembered

I once was a melody
Riddled through the ocean waves.
I could hear the symphony
Of wild things free and brave.

And hauntingly we all remember
Many lifetimes past when we
Could kindle images:
       Our spirits ...
              Infinitely free.

Three dimensions have a way
Of making light my gallantry.
Tamed and funneled, to my displeasure;
Shackled from universal pleasure;
Bound now with a finite measure —

I'm anchored from the wildness of the universal sea.

But hauntingly we all remember
Many lifetimes past when we
Could kindle images:
       Our spirits ...
              Infinitely free.

Transparent Lures

I have known hunger.

From eyes wide with questions
Mouths warm with pleasant suggestions
Hands sweaty, pleading and needy

There have been moments
Beyond thought and action
When desperate hunger surrounded me

Frightened me to mutable stone
Wishing I were still and safe at home

Nectar in a Sieve

No,
I'm not confused.
I'm listening to my heart stir.
I'm reviewing past friendships
    And lovers
    And people of wonder in my life
    And letting them go.

I'm slowly, lovingly saying goodbye to my childhood
    And naivete,
    Which allowed me to feel exhilarating moments.

I'm telling my heart that I needn't long for innocent urgings
    To follow blindly,
Not when there is erotic speed in wisdom
And fathoms of feelings and infinities of emotions.
    That explode deeply ...
    Beneath and around

The singular note that innocence happily bellows.

I can plunge into new moments of life.
By distilling simplicity and inspiration from innocence
That was long-ago fairy tales and sienna childhoods.

A New Face On The Set

It was bright lights and a camera!
Everything was like a show!
They always knew what was best for me
To dress, to act, to go

But I got a wake up call
It carried no whether or when
It came down from deep inside
The message said, "Just follow him."

"Just follow him," but who was this –
The next director on the set?
The only one who had the answers
One I had locked up and kept ...

From listening to.

I squelched his cries
I fed him lies
I closed his eyes
I traded sides
I agonized
I made him hide
And he still loved me deep inside.

And now that all my tricks are up
He's standing up
And throwing up
And seeing love
And being love
And being loved

He moved above
Where action is
To flip the script
To bring me this ...
That I am love

And in control
I own this script!
Lights, camera, roll!

An Unfailed Attempt

By not overspeaking my actions,
I cannot be the one to obscure them.
By drifting without resistance,
I will certainly arrive at foreign shores.

By embracing encounters with my perception of face value
I create my own illusions, dilemmas.

I cannot transpose these.
I cannot decode them.
I cannot find the currency!

But ...
I can take them with me. I will.
I can tuck them into a wrinkle in time. I do.
I can wait for my experiences to claim them. I must....

And they resurface ... as pearls.

Courting Destiny

Even through the glare of wrath
We still move on God's chosen path for us,
And we still share, still laugh
And we are mindful as we ask ...

What have I to recommend me
But myself and my good deeds –
Not just those done long ago
But those accomplished recently?

Who have I to sing my praises
If my life has maladies?

Not just family, who have raised me
But the enemies who could be
Were it not for who I am
And my good deeds.

Brothers

To heal a wound ... I wish I could.
To right a wrong ... I know I should.
To remain unyielding behind a plan
Of respect for life and fellow man.

These things are not beyond my reach
Each day I live, I also teach
By my respect for humble gifts
Dreams can explode beyond my wish.

We all can live in harmony
We can preserve ecology, diversity, and honor our humanity.
We can live well and all live free
But all of this begins with me.

Does this seem too rational?
Is this too international?
Is this just a fantasy?
No!
In my heart the key is me.
We must replace the you with me

A new Manifest Destiny
Of love, respect, and unity.
A righteous brother's philosophy.

Always ...

Always
Beginning classes
Don't ever find
Good happenings.

I just
Keep loose -
Maybe nice opportunities
Pull quickly 'round.

Sometimes this
Upper voice
Whales xerophilous youth's zeal.

Meet Me In NYC

Meet me up in New York City
Just you and your friends and me and mine
Meet me up in New York City.
We'll paint the town up so pretty
Just you and me and them in New York City
And we'll have a real good time.

I want to get away — tired of work
But can't afford to stay off and flirt with losing my job.
I'd really like to go to Paris, Rome or London.
That's just so far from home —
My bank account is undone anyway.

So ...
Meet me up in New York City
Just you and your friends and me and mine.
Meet me up in New York City.
We'll paint the town up so pretty
Just you and me and them in New York City
And we'll have a real good time.

Beacons

of

Love

Love brings out the tenderest feelings - placing songs, ballads, laments, in our hearts. It is here that there is a leveled playing field. Societies have not yet found a way to "genderize" those incredible feelings we all share when we love. We share our love and share in love. Here is the voice of a mother on her own.

Misty

Did you know that your behavior alter greatly when your pulse
Climbs beyond your body heat; it causes you to rush.

Everything around you slows to let you take your time, but still
You seem as though in this sane world you're acting like you just took ill.

And I let a haze surround me so that focus on you is
Even more exacting when your speed sound hastens to a whiz.

When I look you tell me where you are
In this grand, multi-dimension world.
I bet you don't even know your starting mark today
You confuse yourself when you extract you from my play.

And I am not even playing.
I am neutral in my part
Sans the use of script or prop –
Off the cuff ... from my heart.

You make me laugh, but not too hard.
You make me cry, but just not quite.
With you it is that my emotions
Remain frolicksomely light.

I am light and cool
You are heavy heat
Each of us becomes a mist
When our spirits meet.

Phoenix Friend

How is it that you've got a face I know I know,
But I just can't place?
How is it that you've got a face I know I know,
But I just can't place?

Those eyes, those eyes I've seen, I swear
When I was out to sea somewhere.

The same big and brown
The same wide and round

How is it that you know my heart
When we're together or far apart?
How is it that you know my heart
When we're together or far apart?

Your soul speaks to me;
Love you set me free.

How is it that you've got a face I know I know,
But I just can't place?
You're teasing me because you've been
Before time and after — my phoenix friend.

Opposites

You have your own style and I've got mine.
You go your own way and I go mine.
Though we live together, we do fine.
Honey you doing your thing
And me doing mine.

You like your clothes casual and raw.
And I like mine simple, chic and soft.
Our worlds are different — so different but
We hang together like Jeff and Mutt

Painting the town red is fun for me.
You say fun is anywhere that we
Can be together — 'cause you love me.
And I love you truly, truly my sweet.

Pleasant Encounter

I'm such a pleasant encounter
Running in-between continents and such.
You like me better than the others.
I told you that you would like me very much.

How shall I bring it to you baby.
Wrap me up in silk and embroidered lace.
You just don't know how you thrill me
When I see that look upon your face.

And I know why those others
Keep wanting to come to you, boy.
You are the master blaster in everything that you do, boy.

From continent to continent
You look me up from all the others there.
Between your business meetings and mine dear
We still find the time for this love affair.

Who's Chasing Whom

I've been trying to write this song
Ever since I knew
Where my life was heading,
And knowing it was with you

Chances are you didn't know.
How could you guess your plight?
I've been out to get you honey,
Yes, you know I'm right.

Think about it. May be that
You knew but kept it in your hat.
Maybe it's that I was caught
We neither may ever find out ...
Who's chasing whom?

Lock me in a room
And cut out the lights.
Rock me in your arms
Tonight and all my nights

Places that you use to go
I made my point to be
Chasing you was difficult
But you were getting to me

Chances are you didn't know.
How could you guess your plight?
I was out to get you honey,
Yes, you know I'm right.

Think about it. May be that
You knew but kept it in your hat.
Maybe it's that I was caught
We neither may ever find out ...
Who's chasing whom?

Lock me in a room
And cut out the lights.
Rock me in your arms
Tonight and all my nights

Chances are you didn't know.
How could you guess your plight?
I was out to get you honey
Yes, you know I'm right.

Reality

You may search my love your whole lifetime
And never find reality
But oh my love for one last night
Stay here with me.

Darling I had searched all time untold
Trying to learn what life's about
And until we met I was uncertain
I had my doubts.

Was it true that life's a great box of candy

All wrapped up shiny and new
Or was life just an apple on a tree
To leave the world in blues.

They say that if you seek you will find
Answers to what you must know.
I have spent my hours seeking in the darkness,
Searching for a candle,
Reaching for a rainbow.

And now I find what I was looking for in you.

So if we must part, know I'll haunt your heart
Because there's one truth you've got to see
That no matter where you search you will find
Our reality comes back to you and me
Together, forever, eternally.

Passing Time

Just passing time together you and me
Spending our time together everyday
Let others party in the evening time
Come be beside me in the twilight.

You, darling, are what I need tonight
Where have you been all of my life?

Just passing time together you and me
Spending our time together everyday
Yours is a smooth mellow personality
Ooh wee! Ooh wee! Ooh wee!

In our fantasy, we can make a perfect world
You be my man, and I'll be your only girl.

Just passing time together you and me
Spending our time together everyday
You, my darling, are what I need tonight.
Where have you been all my life?

Let's take love slow;
Let's make it so;
Let's make love grow ...
Seal all our tomorrows.

Just passing time ...
Just passing time ...
Just passing time ...

Complete

A momentary lapse
When I could not recall
The easy way you please me
How you charge me when you see me

Simple state of confusion
From my point of view
So complete your love is sweetness
I thought I was you.

Tell me what you told me when you told me that you cared
The time, the space I spent with you
I had forgot we'd shared
I think I wrapped you 'round my finger,
Bound you to my heart, and

You swore the sun would melt the stars
Before you'd let us part

Simple state of confusion
From my point of view
So complete your love is sweetness
I thought I was you.

Summer Madness

Your open arms and I'm coming in.
You smile at me and I'm going again.
And you wonder how come.
How come?
How come?

Sun in our faces, shining for us
Step up the pace; life's waiting for us
'Cause I think I know how come ...
How come ...
How come.

It's summer madness. Here comes the sun.
Clear skies are promises our day has come
It's never raining; when we're together.
We bring the sun that chases bad weather.
It's summer madness. Here comes the sun.

You and your guitar
Me and my songs
Let's take the next jet
Head for the sun
Let the world wonder how come.
How come?

How come?

It's summer madness. Here comes the sun.
We'll dry the tears, clear them all from the sky.
We'll paint it azure as we glide on by.
It's summer madness. Here comes the sun.
It's summer madness.
We are the sun.

No Recovery

Did I hurt your feelings
When you ricocheted mine off the wall?
I could hear your scream
When you could not hear me at all.

Little things like "Come inside."
While pushing me away
Caused an awful sound effect.
The decibels have not been met
Since hard rock came into high-tech

And I have not recovered yet.

Did I make you nauseous
From the fatal cut you made that bled?
I could see the sweat bead up
And roll from your forehead.

You didn't see me bleed inside
Because you walked away
The cutting thought of our love dead
Left me with hurt and passions red

But that "We're through," is all you said.

And I have not recovered yet.

Write Me

Far from reach, but in my heart
Just a breach; we're not apart

If you just write me, write me; write me.

You keep in touch the way you said.
Send me sweet thoughts to fill my head —

If you just write me; write me; write me.

Waiting here day after day
Told you I would, I'm here to stay.
Let me know when you're coming home —
Maybe tomorrow, that's not too soon.

I got a letter yesterday
And even though we're miles away
I get a warm feeling right here in my heart
When you write me; write me ... write me.

The Chill of Loneliness

Sitting here and freezing too
I didn't get a call from you
Replacing warmth
The cold air passes
Through my wounded heart

It's funny how your pleasant face
Your self-contained, confident grace
Your agile and athletic gait
Has me falling apart

Don't laugh, I'm sure you've things to do
Cause I'm a busy person too
But I know that I haven't pulled you close as I would like
Or you'd be on the telephone
You wouldn't leave me so alone
You'd get right up and
You would dial my number every night.

Going Fishing

Once in love always in love I told him I'd be.
But I did him wrong, and now he's through with me.
I broke his heart.
Now he's broke mine.
He set me free, cut me loose from his line.

And he told me,
"I'm going fishing, fishing to find a love of my own.
You played me one time too many wrongs.
Fishing, fishing to find a love of my own.

There's more than one fish for me in this pond."

Time slowly went by, but I could not let him go.
'Cause I still cared, and I know that he knows.
So yesterday we met right at the bay
Fish weren't biting, we decided
Apart and alone just wasn't our way.

So no more fishing, fishing
Our hearts have found their way home.
In love together we have no reason to roam.
Fishing, fishing, our days of fishing are done.
We've other love games to play in the sun.

Ascension

When finally we burst to the top
No one will be surprised.
It will have been a steady climb
We've reached with open eyes.

My love and I will find our way
A single path
That runs beside a sultry stream
A brook that laughs
The ripples of a thousand pleasures
We have found
By treading forward steadily
On fertile ground.

The love that rolls from inner depths
We with each and others share
Rejoicing in the joy it gives
To give to all our all in care.

Panting while in deep blue, frosted warm nights with each other
We become our own protectors, children, siblings, lovers, father, mother
And the days will find us disciplined, at ease,
Drenched with fragrant sunshine, universal peace.

Late Summer Storm

Peaceful, isn't this the place where you want to be?
Cozy, just the mood, the music, and just you and me
Now shall we discuss that little argument last night?
I've forgotten it already; you're the only thing in sight.

But let me check your temperature.
You're feeling rather warm.
I know how to cool you though in this late summer storm.

Just a few sweet, sweet kisses on your brow.
Tell me darling; tell me honey; how does that feel now?
Lover would you like to have a cool, refreshing drink?
Ease your fears? Tell me about this storm and what you think?

Am I tired? I'm never tired of wisdom you impart.
Thrilling how the night alarms when the lightening starts.
So willingly your arms protect me and embrace my heart.

Lightening that enflames the sky is nothing next to this.
I can't seem to catch my breath under your stormy kiss.

And sweetheart have I told you that you're feeling rather warm.
Oh – I know how to cool you though in this late summer storm.

Confessions of the Accused

We're adults, so I confess
Others have felt this same way
They couldn't stay for they knew best
As my main attraction - they each fell prey

Though hurts - I labored long to mend
And though love I freely gave
Anxiously they felt that I ...
I'd rob their souls
Just like a knave.

My heart could never hold them back
Or even plead for them stay.
My heart would stop.
My voice would crack
But I would let them walk away.

And though I never try to hold
Love close that I hold dear to me
Although my love – deep as the sea.
Although my love – strong as the storms
Although my love – eternally
Forever loves with open arms
I can't ...
I won't ... commit such robbery.

Again ...

When I was eighteen we were here
With passions in flame
All I could do was dance ...
And sing...
Shudder ... and cry out at each little encounter

Because we were new
Not to the world, but to me.

And I was soft
Not to my mind, but to my heart.

It didn't notice the stealthy exchange and contrasts:
The ebbing of childhood's soft, quiet pastels for
The rush and hard brilliance of
Bountiful, backbreaking, ball-busting life

Life's amorphous blend swelled into my psyche
Reverberated from the inside out
Resounded with laughter, screams, and sharp, jagged edges —
Just this side of the pitch and decibel that shatters vessels

Decades have passed
And we again are here
Our passions in flame

And I can dance
And sing
Shudder ... and cry out at each little encounter
Because I am this soft
That can finally absorb
The shock that once curled around me long ago
And arrested my vulnerability

And paralyzed my momentum
And suspended my faith
And created, fortified, and polished
A sheath around me
That so closely resembled me
That only I knew because
I felt it explode, melt, drip like syrup and dissolve
As we again are here.

Returns to Puppy Love

Puppy love, how aptly named
To love and linger without shame
To laugh in bliss when problems seem ...

To just be shadows - darkened stains,
Residual mockings from the sun

When heartbreak is a distant shore
Its waves recede from your front door
They clear your path and fasten more ...

To lives left hanging — now forgotten
On the clotheslines in the sun.

But even still I hurry, yet
To memories I can't forget
To puppy fantasies which ratchet ...
Needed courage as I'm tethered
Without shade and burning in the sun.

So puppy love embers burn bright
And counter my heart's sun-seared blight

Until love rushes in again ...

As a new day —balanced by rain
And nurtured by the sun

Nemesis?

★

Vanquish Them.

Xenophobes have much to gain by self-aggrandizing statements, superhuman claims, narrow boundaries for acceptance of others, and professing to be the standard by which everyone else must be measured. Beguiling tactics such as simplistic visions of material wealth and romanticized adventures of war dwarf the value of relationships that must frequently be postponed or sacrificed if a man is to arrive as a "real man." Wealth and adventures are the matter of stories children hear and long for. But who is there to tell them to our daughters and sons, explain the pitfalls and shortcuts, and protect them each night when fathers, captive to their own myths, have been spirited away? Absent fathers may leave behind them a legacy of misguided values.

J. W. Doncan

Help Me ... For Now

Help me for now while I struggle baby
Then set me free.
Stick with me baby 'till I reach the top
Then don't get trampled by me.

'Cause I can make it
And when I do
You can call it
Your victory.

'Cause you can watch as I
Tell everyone
How single-handedly I
Moved the earth
How I made my way
All alone
Without a soul in my corner
Without a friend
To call my own.

For now give me that reassurance again
That you love me.
Tell me and show me how special I am.
Love me, then move.
I'd never hurt you
Not you baby
When I make my final move.

But you can watch as I
Tell everyone
How single-handedly I
Moved the earth
How I made my way

All alone
Without a soul in my corner
Without a friend
To call my own.

You look at me I want for you to see
A look of fame.
With all the power, wealth,
The recognition and
The love it brings.
But I won't make it baby
Not without you
And when we get there
Please don't forget where
You laid down your
Walking shoes.

I'd never hurt you
Not you baby
When I make my
Final move.

But you can watch as I
Tell everyone
How single handedly I
Moved the earth
How I made my way
All alone
Without a soul in my corner
Without a friend
To call my own.

Help me for now while I struggle baby
Then set me free.
Stick with me baby 'till I reach the top
Then don't get trampled by me.

The Boss' Luxury

Easy for you to say
  That a drum is a hollow
  That you beat with a stick
  And the band members follow

  That time is a thing
  With dainty feet
  She keeps me in step
  As I walk down the street.

Easy for you to say
  That I go in circles
  You walk a straight line
  Carrying messages
  But I just keep time
Easy for you to say
  If you make the rules
  Then it's easy for you
  To name all the fools.

Competition's Complications

Does your narrow definition mean
I must match this sham to be a man?
Do you think what you think of me
Really changes who I am?

As I strive to be more who I am
You strive to be what others want
Doesn't that make me more of a man?
By definition — you a pawn?

I comfort a friend who is crying, then ...
If she is a woman, I'm a real man?
If I am a woman and she is one too ...
Am I as a nurturer to my sex true?

If I am a woman and he is a man then ...
Am I a bitch and he a mere sham?
If we are both men, then are we way gay?
These boxes are prisons if I choose to stay!

But I love to defy what it is that you "know."
It frees me up, and it helps you grow.

Stretching out for happiness
I'll spin and strike like shards of sun ...
Search and singe such elements
As needed to bring clarity
To my dimensions — one by one.

But I'll keep in mind your criticism
Though its goal is to rid me as competition.

Pseudo-International Dilettante

Trans-World Aura
      This man:
      A European collar
      An intellectual air

A *hungry, hungry* stare.

Surrounds himself with power
    So as:
    To kindly camouflage
    In this his finest hour
    His wealthy entourage

The means by which we measure men
Are foolish standards he's surpassed.

The gold, cuff-links
The toothy grin
Are featured as the sun zeniths
And then so swiftly passed.

"So foolish!"
    What he thinks of those
    Who dwell on fancy thoughts of love
How can love be a state of bliss
Compared to wealth, power and all this?

Rejoicing his all in his mind
All else for him — a waste of time.

Beyond Home

We balance our callings
For our loved ones and our homes.
The distant whispers draw us to
An abyss of unknown

The tightrope we tread skillfully
From throttling routines
Of quicksand - dulling senses

Clogging eyes, ears, throats, and dreams.

We cross uneasy inches (snaking power lines, detached)
To search for whispered promises — unparalleled, unmatched.
Below sharp shards await us, dare our padding efforts slip
Beyond abyss the promise holds us with a steady grip.

We find there is another side
Of years from tearing free.
Hearts racing with such eagerness
For shortly we shall see.
Does the promise disappoint us?
It's excitement there we seek.

And we see the greens, the blue, blue skies,
        Activity we've craved.
As we near we'll find new sights
        New sounds, new faces like ours — brave.
As we focus on the thrill of the new hearts and hands to hold
It is more than we expected. It is more than we were told.
It is more than we projected.
        Dazzling, sparkling, beauteous, gold!
It is smooth, and crystal clear and cool, refreshing as the rain.
And it looks faintly familiar like a family portrait - framed.
Now the faces all are detailed. I can see without a strain.

It's a mirror of our families
Those we left in search of gain.

An American Horizon

Glittering rock – blasted up, frozen
It's an American horizon,
      Yes!

Ant tinkerers, miners.
Inside golden halos.
Live drama, pathos.
Tilting with wind blows.
Scuttling under thick snows:
Dense fallout remnants from world-money throws

Glittering rock – blasted up, frozen
It's an American horizon,
      Yes.

Ant tinkerers, miners.
Inside golden halos.
Live drama, pathos.
Tilt with the wind blows.
Creep from the thick snows:
Suffocating fallout vapors from
Emboldened, egregious, satiated – those.

Glittering rock – blasted up, frozen
It's an American horizon,
Yes?

In Praise of
All Our
Moms

Real men love their moms though sons' expressions may be thwarted by society's penchant for nurturing insensitivity. And moms' determination to keep paths open for their sons, especially without the support of fathers, is a formidable task and for a rapidly growing number. This under-appreciated population of mothers on their own are celebrated because they are under-acknowledged, at times the brunt of jokes, and usually working without flash or cash. Without our community moms, many success stories would not exist. Moms on their own deserve praise.

Thank You

Dear Mom,
When we were too little to know ...
You held our hands and walked us safely to new places.
You spoke words of encouragement and inspiration.
You demonstrated integrity and loyalty.
You reflected beauty and vision.
You hugged us and kissed us and fed us.
You spoke to us, sang to us, read to us.
You did all of this until we understood
That we were worth respect and love.

But never once did you speak of your worth
Or the respect and love you deserve.
And so I will speak them to you ...

Mothers do not have to protect their children or even try to keep them
from harm, but you did. They do not have to acknowledge their children's
fragile sense of ability. Mothers are not required to remain ardent
supporters and fans of their children — even when we make mistakes in
front of our mothers' eyes.

But you led us to understand that we have the ability to make real the
visions we have in our minds. And even as you have blinked back your
fears, you helped us to what it was that we wanted. And when others
have draped themselves in the luxuries at their fingertips, you walked
past them to buy something you felt would be useful to us.

These are not small, isolated things that you did. You wrapped these
overtures, gestures, words, and actions in love, enthusiasm, and passion.
And today you peacefully sit, not asking for the world — though mom,
you gave it to us. We love you, will always love you, respect you, and
cherish you for this.

Mother 12.98

God is watching as you tenderly are sprouting:
Boldy beautiful and startlingly sweet
From the earth you drew
Hardiness, a vibrant hue,
And protective thorns that serve you,
And an air that draws us to you,
So with wonderment we gather at your feet.

Yet a rose is not your name.

Smitten as one is
When cupid's bow's aquiver:
Revealing whispers and a racing heart
Even all of this cannot deliver
Passions for us that you feel
And the love that you impart

Yet love is not your name.

Sought and coveted
In a material world
Lustfully it's gathered
And unwillingly it's shared.
Though its sun-like brilliance
Can create such opulence
Your faith — a precious metal
So, like gold — it too is rare.

Yet gold is not your name.

But you represent them well, Mom.
With Rose's sensuality,
Love's deepest blushing passion,

And Faith as rare as gold,
You represent them all, Mom
They won't die; they won't grow old
They won't fade throughout the years
They'll live on in us, your children
Through our lives and through our souls
An eternity of years.

A Love Story

This is a love story
About a young lady
Whose love through the years
Has remained steadfast — bravely.

When I could not see
Could not care for my safety
She held me and fed me
And she kept me warm.

And when I was scared
By life's unending challenges
She like a tree
Sheltered me from the storm.

The days and she labored
The nights and she prayed
I'll never repay
Sacrifices she made.

The hurts that she mended
The broken hearts tended
The wounds that she healed
While her own she concealed.

Mama.

Aunty 4.80

Let our minds
Record the times
Of endless seasons
Melted into rhymes or
Meaningful prose of feeling
Finely woven into sturdy, well-made songs.

And they ring in my mind
Like a choir's full, rhythmic echoing voices.
Laughing on ...
Singing on ...

Sing me those songs of family and friends
For encouragement.
Sing them to me when I am alone..
Let me hear them filling my head
With high pitched notes of birds and warm breezes

Let me hear the earthy tenors
Laughing and playing with my mind
Encouraging me by reliving the joyous notes
Of family past.

Give me hot and heavy that solid base
That nurturing base from which my spirit draws its fire.

I can hear them
All in the songs of my family
That you sing to me.
These songs are locked forever in my soul.

Aunty Emily

Who is the lady who sits by the window
And patiently, daily awaits my return

While Mama is working and Daddy whose ego
Enlarged, forces shirking of familial chores?

It's my Mama's sister who used to tend Mama
Who sits at attention protective and kind.

Aunty! She gathered her strength of survival
And lavishly lathered me with what she'd learned.

She forced me by filling my head with enticements
To choose to be willing to surpass the scores.

And to strive for excellence no matter what my path
She helped me be my best in my own time.

Loyalty led her for three generations
To always be there, stalwart and firm.

Watching each face go by 'till the day's over
'Till she hears the footsteps I pat on the floor

And my mama's sister, who used to tend Mama
Is pleased with my gifts to her: patience, love, time.

Big Sis / Mother Earth

Mother Earth ...
Satisfying the needs of the multitudes
Big Sis ...

As Mother Earth, do what you have to do.

And that is to cry when we cry,
And that is to laugh when we do,
And that is for tearful eyes that you dry
And moments you share (and you do want to too.)

You appear where we walk. You respond when we talk
You understand all as long as it falls
In the seasons of time
Of the earth as you climb
To reach down and out to more of the crowd
Because as you listen — one voice is your mission
To hear it and fasten it onto your dress hem ...

As Mother Earth!
Carrying out the advice of the multitudes.
And you Girl
Must do — just what you were born to do.

So ...
You absorb the heartbeat of our nation
You transmit it's message without distortion
And you do so wherever you're stationed
And to each you impart a fair portion

And you wet the whistle; you whet the mind
You receive information — distill and refine
And people will come as they must do
To hear Mother Earth and get "talked to."

So Mother Earth ..
Pour us a nourishment.
Mother Earth
We'll drink, relax, and talk a bit.

And Mother Earth
You'll flourish from it
Because you're an integral part of it

Mother Earth
You're in your element.

Now I Lay Me Down to Sleep

Now I lay me down to sleep
And I will try hard not to weep
For those whose ruptured rest replaces
Peaceful dreams of loving faces
And who wake tired and worn
Rest required — not met at morn.

I pray the Lord my soul to keep
Along with those whose tired feet
Cannot pause to ease the pain
Of overtired, swollen veins
And puffy ankles, wobbling knees
Backs whose aches are never eased

If I should die before I wake
God will have carried me to a fate
Some older sisters would gladly meet
For death to steal each from her sleep
When tired limbs and eyes that burn
Cause restless nights, each tossed and turned.

I pray the Lord, my soul, to take
Self pity that causes my core to shake

And to forget my sisters' plight
Of weary limbs and restless nights
Let strength and patience guide my sight
Or take me too within this night.

Tribute

God, everyday help me to say
In all I do for others
A little prayer sent everywhere
As a tribute to my mother.

And in the future some cold day
As I watch mothers pass my way
I hope that I can smile and say
I treated Mother well.

There're moms I know who covet their vice.
They live in the bottle -- roll with the dice.
Their time's too great a sacrifice
To spend with a small child.

Their anger, just to think of it
To stay at home and baby-sit
Raging, makes them want to spit.
And children can't compel

A mother's love, care, or concern
They're on their own; they have to learn
To outside sources, children turn
To dangers menacing and wild.

The moms who've never known their children
Late in life wish they had reared them

Too, too late — and now they fear them.
Moms need their offspring now.

While in their youth they had no time
To mend a hurt, to shape a mind.
A party was a better kind
Of way to while the hours.

So in the winter of their lives
These moms, they speak with pleading eyes
Because they know that all their cries
Won't even raise a brow.

My mom, who works from sun to sun
Still claims that her work is not done
'Till her grandson is grown and strong.
Her time's not hers, but ours.

I am so grateful everyday
I know there is no way to pay
Her for the youth she toiled away
To help me have a life.

Single-handedly she had
The work of both a mom and dad.
And even with cash thinly stretched,
She never showed regret

For work that she felt must be done
To feed and clothe, and teach her young.
Her standards were too high, by some.
But this was not their strife.

God bless my mom for loving me
For caring and for teaching me

For sharing and beseeching me
To be my very best

We Gather 'Round You

Fire flame
Quick with heat
Red with laughter
Run from rain.

Never fair
Chasing leaves
Children gather
Dancing there.

Crowding close
We all love you
You're our light
So we pose.

Fire flame
We surround you
Feeling warmth ...

Sometimes pain.

Our Mothers' Hearts

When everything is shaky,
Fear is breaking us apart
We reach out to our Mothers' hands
And feel the calmness in their hearts

Golden flecks strengthen their hearts.
Nerves of pearls and diamond dust.
Their oceans all envelope us
With compassion, wisdom, love.

They have raised us ...

And stood by us ...

For as long as we have been
On this turtle island rock.

We love you dearest Mom
And friend.

The Finish
Gives Meaning
to the Race

A ny slice into the lives of fatherless men reveals a mother -
working and praying behind the scenes, observing and searching for
inroads through society's well-laid barricades. The end of the race will
answer the questions they dare not stop their work to examine. Mothers-
on-their-own work to let the finish exonerate their efforts and the efforts
of their sons.

A Mother's Desperation

I'll pull my sunshine
    From the skies
From my son's smile
    And his dark eyes
From my mom's meals
    And children's squeals.

I'll pull my sunshine from the fray
    To help me make it through the day,
        God help me make it one more day.

Untouchable

It's cold outside
And rainy too
The wind is blowing
Through and through
But it can never touch my heart
For there inside is you!

Tomorrow's Painful Joy

A little man ...

> His hands fit gently within my hands
> But as I lead him I'm aware
> That for all of my love and care
> He must still grow to reject all this
> Once consenting hands become fists
> Gently bent to toil at work
> His dynamic vistas from inert.

His hands will toil toward visions not my own.

> Those wondrous eyes that tear and cry
> When mama scolds and will not dry
> I know as time does tick away
> That they must learn to never stray
> From paths that this new man creates
> To beckon his future: his bright new day.

His tears will be for joy and joy alone.

> The slender arms wrapped 'round my neck
> Must lengthen, thicken, and caress
> The life and love of this new man
> And as I hold his little hand
> Upon my heart right now and stand
> Tomorrow he'll stand strong and kind
> With a man's wisdom, grace, and mind
> Tomorrow he will understand ...

When he is fully grown.

Lessons

I turned my child's face to the sun to teach him to look for the light.
I sent him to fetch a very old debt to teach him to fight for his rights.
I sent him to school on a mission to teach him to strive for his dreams.
My son is a man of the world and prepared with the use of these few
precious things.

Enigma

You stand firm in mellowed passion, dreamy
Your presence sophisticated, seamy
You are a determined, quiet fire
Consumed on the pyre, you return from the mire
Your thoughts consume yet remain detached
Your reason unparalleled, unmatched
Your spirit peaceful, laced with tremors
Your being — solid earth and wind-blown glitter
You're symmetry and a bit more
Your feelings erupt within your core
You speak with a soul bereft of deception
You carefully avoid formal reception
While my eyes question every thought
Yours is a battle won not fought.

I Sit, 11. 01 ...

I sit,
The monitor's glare highlighting my face,
Drawing silhouettes behind me.
Danny's laughter flashes.

Inadequately,
Words on the screen earthquake my continuum of emotions.
Danny clicks the phone down and yells, "Mom, where are the cookies you bought?
      ... You didn't eat them all up did you?"

I laugh and continue with the ideas in front of me
That I know must materialize
Before images sink so deep in my heart that
I can't untangle them from the rest of who I am.
Blunt, boyish footsteps thunder down the stairs,
Jilting my balanced concentration:
A mother's skill — listening and planning.

So many feelings ...
So many feelings compressed into secondary communications:
Watered down words.
Just words
Though carefully carved out
Are still sterile
Even with yet another final revision.

A big hug to Danny now that he is such a big boy,
A man really — 18 years old
And in college.
One last, "I love you. I miss you Danny,"
Carefully written message
Efficiently disappears from the monitor as quickly as did
Danny's "See-you-in-December" smile
Laser itself into my heart.
With one month to go
Danny regularly travels the back streets of my consciousness.

Gentle

Think in terms of gentle things
For your gentle soul.
You are such a gentle man
Who needs a gentle hand to hold.

Somewhere There Is You

Ocean depths can rob the soul
Arrest the heart - freeze it cold.
When I'm tossed like a ship at sea
Waiting for anyone to rescue me,

I'm buoyed by peace and solitude
As I set my mind's eye on you.
I'm washed in warmth and happiness
Knowing somewhere that the world is blessed ...
          My son with you.

February Hugs '97

When you see my son hug him for me.
          I'll see him before you do,
                    And I'll tell him the things I want him to know.

I'll tell him that I love him
More than the rest of my precious days in this life.

I'll tell him that I'm trying my best
To make sure he has the opportunities
To live up to his own brand of success,
And that I'm trying to make sure that
His options continue to blossom.

I'll tell him that his unique blend of
Stubbornness, innovation, intelligence, compassion,
And vision are continuing to evolve.

And if he remains faithful to his dreams ...
           Unshaken in his belief in himself ...
                  His feet will barely skim the surface of the earth
                        As he directs his own controlled hydroplane
                              Into the future.

If you hug him for me ...
 He'll never be without the love
        I want him to feel from me,

        But from you
        He won't wince at the fears I have
        From so many dangers I see in this world.
        They are blended into my hugs.

He'll never be without the caress of closeness
        I want him to feel with me,

        But from you
        He won't have the shock of hollowness
        That our society repeatedly
        Shoots through our attempts at communicating
        Now that he is
        Establishing himself as a man.

He'll never be without the warmth
        I want him to feel from me,

        But from you
        It won't be scorching with a love so intense

That it defies intrusion,
That might repel a love in his life that he must have
As a man.

Hug him for me, and when you do
My son will never be without my love
    In this world
    Because my love is as big as this world
    But from you
    It will not pass on fears
    That he will learn all too soon on his own.

And when my son feels that he has become a man
I will be able to hug him again
    And again
        And again
            And again ...

Forever Regulus

You rise like the grass
Though trampled it returns each spring
You move like the wind
Through obstacles it learns to sing
You share like the sun
Which never has refused to shine
You're as great as all God's gifts
You're part of a divine design.
You know like the ocean knows
It's depths and floor hold no surprise
You accept the knowledge that's

Beyond our sight and of the skies
You point out your visions to your listeners —
To all of us ...

For your's is the Star of Kings
Your totem is the Regulus.

All Pathways

Son as you traverse journeys on your own
You know God in your heart is who you need.
And God's Light at your feet to wisdom leads,
And that all pathways lead you home to God.

A Continuum

Knowledge does not replace wisdom
    They go hand in hand.
        Listen to your elders, my sons
            In time you'll understand.

Danny's Music '98

Music is a universal language
    That transcends our speech
        And thought
            And time.

And it harmonizes with
    Our bodies' true desires.
        It can reignite a soul
            Or rekindle a worn spirit

> Our attraction draws us near it
> Like a pattern to a rhyme.

You, my son, are an ancient spirit:
Stardust, eternal, in an infinite twilight.

Music is one of your animations.
Let it spread the wisdom
Of your presence
With its light.

Continue to be true to you
In everything you do.

Let your music and desires
Warm us with passionate fires

And all else my son
Will fall
In place
In time.

Bless You

God Bless You Son ...
Bless your every little bone

From your bass guitar
To your baritone
From your morning dragon breath
To your evening sweet cologne

And I know that
God will always help you fly high on your own
And bring you safely home.

On Turning 21

Some say at the age of twenty-one
That a man is what young males become.
But I know a man who — without a dad —
Was a man long before twenty-one.

And it's you my son who has struggled along
Sometimes with no light up ahead.
But you keep your eyes on your vision of God
Even through rocky roads that you tread.

You've struggled on upward my son
Through your fear, ever clear-headed,
Focused and strong.
Though your road has had twists in it, pits in it,
And it's been steep,
And God knows that it's long.

And my son you've come far
From your Regalus Star
And your life is revealing its truth.
As you steady your charted course,
Welcome God's wind in your sails
And while still in your youth!

You have known all along,
Though your mother's hands - strong
And as loyally poised at your oars
Sometimes slip, or ache, or must rest,

Or they shake,
But when God mans your sails - your ship soars.

As you fly through a windless night
Facing oncoming storms
Knowing that darkness is just before dawn,
Though your mom whispers in your ear,
God assuages your fear,
Co-pilots and guides you on.

If your words fail to say
What your heart must convey
When your passions, though varied,
Long to be known,
Words sometimes miss their mark,
But the music you make
Is God's gift to touch hearts
Far and near with your songs.

So whether you see God as Buddha or Yaweh
A captain, a pilot, or as your guitar
Unexplainable vision that guides your decisions
At your young age shows who you are.

'Cause a man isn't something one graduates to
Isn't something proclaimed or bestowed,
Not a size, nor a sound, nor a gesture, an age,
Nor a phrase, nor a look of his clothes.

And so many males who like you,
Waiting for fathers to give them one word
To encourage them on,
Find their God-light within.
They themselves become men.
And like you, son, before twenty-one.

And little boys, yes,
Need the blessings of their dads
As urgently as little girls.
But they cry to themselves as the world lies,
    "Men ...Tears are mistaken
        And they must be quelled!"

Baby boys like their sisters are observant,
Sensitive, discriminating and equally kind.
But boys labor to reap for society
Egregious financial heaps as they die inside
And bestow all to elite
While the process defeats their humanity ...
All while it guts their sweet hearts
And it blunts their fine minds.

Why do some say that men should never cry?
Not I! Where would all their tears go? Collected to water
The gardens of sycophants' wealth
And pretend — as they're taught — not to know!

A man is a flesh and blood human
Whose feelings are fragile and sturdy as mine,
Who is not an object; a strong back, a wallet,
Or somebody's one time "good time."
I'm your mom and I've seen
Lots of want-to-be men
Who agonize over their face to the world.
Discouraging empathy, preempting sympathy, while breeding fear,
isolation, hostility.

Afraid to ask for the love or the help they need
Afraid to heed what ties them to humanity
Afraid to look inside, be what they're born to be.

Not just an age, nor a gesture, a phrase
That when spoken a title's bestowed
No, not an intent; no, not an attitude,
And not a look of their clothes.

A flesh and blood human,
Selective, and sensitive,
Letting the God within reveal your path,
You are a man who has long been a man
Before twenty-one years ever passed.

Your road may be rocky;
The waves may be crashing;
The storms may rattle the skies.
But my son you hold on
To your path to your future;
Your vision is through God's own eyes.

I'm proud to be trusted as your friend and mom; to love you,
To sometimes smooth your youthful brow.
And though we're not perfect,
And none of us are,
I couldn't be prouder of you than right now.

I am, I have always been, and I will always be
Proud as your mom, Dearest Danny, my son.
You've proven time and again
Wisdom
And vision
And all this before twenty-one.

And 'cause your sweet smile
Warms me deep like the sun,
I'm stretching the stanzas of this lengthy poem.

It would have been only twenty, my son,
For your smile it is now twenty-one.

Community and
Educator
Discussions

Discussions

GIVE THE FATHERLESS BOY SOME ELBOW ROOM
I'll Tell You A Story ...

Facts

1. What conflict arises for the main character in this poem?
2. What is the reason for the conflict?
3. How is the conflict resolved?

Issues

1. Are the issues in this poem of greater, lesser, or the same importance regardless of one's gender?
2. Does society put greater significance on these issues depending on one's gender?
3. Name several conflicts that you believe are more gender specific? Why would this be?

Bounce

Facts

1. What environmental elements are used in this poem as a source of conflict to "battle"?
2. What solution is offered as a remedy for the conflict?
3. What assumption does the poet make about the main character in giving this advice? So what age group would this character most likely be? Why?

Issues

1. What battles, what fears are prominent today that would require such encouragement?
2. Are there ever times when one should cut his/her losses and admit defeat?
3. Is this type of encouragement more appropriate for sons than daughters? What kinds of monsters are individuals capable of creating in their minds? Explain.

You Are Not Your Father

Facts

1. Why do people use the phrase, "Like father, like son"? Is their any truth to this, or is this only physical appearance and learned behavior? What does this poet feel about this phrase?
2. What behaviors do you believe could have a genetic link and cause a young person to question his ancestry and their impact on him?
3. What is meant by "life is what you make it"? Is this true?

Issues

1. It goes without saying that every person is his own man or her own woman, but what additional significance does this phrase carry with boys whose fathers may not be in the household?
2. This poem indicates that it is one's own decision to burn bridges or not. Is an individual's decision-making inherited or learned? Give examples.
3. The idea of unique or wondrous "gifts" is mentioned. What are gifts an individual may have that are not inherited? What gifts may be inherited?

Never Let them Tell You Who You Are

Facts

1. What characteristics does this poet indicate may be those selected to identify "real men"?
2. What characteristics does this poet indicate are nurtured in a fatherless household?
3. What defense does this poet suggest as a tactic for those who would try to tell you who you are?
4. What personality does this poet assign to those who would try to tell you who you are?

Issues

1. In what ways does our society tell young men who they are?
2. Are there some who are more likely to attempt to tell individuals who they are than others? Why would this be?
3. Are there times when telling an individual who he is, is useful? If so, when?

The Universe Whispers Weapons

Facts

1. What weapons does this child possess, even before the suggestions are given to him by his mother? What additional weapons does his mother suggest?
2. What must this child be prepared to fight? What is his goal?
3. Who does the mother say demonstrates use of these weapons most expertly?

Issues

1. How can these weapons have the power to transform the conditions of black children?
2. How can such gentle ways of behaving in this world be converted into weapons?
3. What are the transformative effects of love, resolve, patience, and remembrance in nature?

OUR VIGILANTLY INDEPENDENT SONS

Two Generations At Breakfast

Facts

1. What is the setting, and who are the characters in this poem?
2. What is the conflict of the poem and the characters' reactions?
3. Does the interaction in this poem seem superficial or honest? Quote the segment that conveys this message. What is the remaining feeling left at the end of the poem? Explain.

Issues

1. In what ways can individuals be from "four corners of the world," other than four geographic locations?
2. In the second stanza, passion is inhibiting appropriateness. Why does passion occasionally become a barrier between individuals?
3. Is it possible to work through a quelled attempt at intimacy? How could this be achieved with school mates, work associates or family?

The Lake
Facts
1. What are the troubles of the speaker and the speaker's actions to deal with them?
2. What are the benefits sought from this lake?
3. What does the lake offer that other friends may not?

Issues
1. How does it benefit society to attach greater concern or disdain to the act of crying, depending on one's gender? Does it?
2. Are the qualities of the lake those that are more appropriate for a specific gender? Why? Why not?
3. What other qualities do we look for in friends?

Train
Facts
1. What is the conflict in this poem?
2. What anchors seem to be missing in the life of this character?
3. Describe the character behind the words with supports from the poem?

Issues
1. What makes a train an appealing form of escape? What are the benefits?
2. What in our lives determines which type of escape to use?
3. What circumstances have ever caused you to feel the same as the speaker in this poem?

Prehension
Facts
1. What is "prehension"?
2. In this dramatic poem, who is meant by "you" in line 6?
3. How does the person in the poem see the world?

Issues
1. This poem is made up of several gestures of kindness. In our society, how are such gestures of kindness usually recognized?
2. Why does our society respond differently, as it does, to large infrequent kindnesses and small daily acts of kindness?

3. Is it important to distinguish between the kindnesses of prayer and small gesture of kindness? Why?

Perennial Weather

Facts

1. What is the speaker telling us?
2. Does this poem speak of internal or external weather? What in the poem leads you to your understanding?
3. To what does the term "couplement" refer?

Issues

1. Is it possible to live one's life without experiencing anger? Is there benefit to experiencing anger?
2. Do women and men react differently when they are angry?
3. Is there a difference between men and women in their frequency, ways and reasons for complimenting? If so, why?

Past Remembered

Facts

1. Is the poem a commentary about reincarnation, stages in one's life, or both? Tie your reasons to the text. What else could this poem be discussing?
2. Are there human actions that aren't bound by dimensions? What would they be?
3. What are the 3 dimensions in which we live? In what ways do 3 dimensions anchor us from "wildness"?

Issues

1. In what way can wildness appear to be brave? Is there truly bravery in wildness? What wild acts can be considered brave?
2. What are three gallant acts performed by men today?
3. Gallantry is a term usually associated with heroic acts that are displayed by men. Are there such acts that are also displayed by women? Why, or why not? What would these be called?

Transparent Lures
  Facts
    1. What type/s of hunger could this be?
    2. When does hunger become frightening?
    3. What type of activity is there beyond thought and action?
  Issues
    1. Is this type of hunger experienced by one gender more frequently?
    2. Are boys typically safe from the sexual hunger that exists in our society?
    3. What reasons make our society more protective of girls?

Nectar in a Sieve
  Facts
    1. What is the speaker in this poem letting go of, and how is that transition playing out?
    2. What new values is the speaker grasping?
    3. What is the speaker now looking forward to?
  Issues
    1. Why does childhood appear more joyous than adulthood? Is this actually so?
    2. Would our lives be happier if we all could remain in our childhoods?
    3. Why is there confusion sometimes during our transitions from childhood to adulthood?

A New Face on the Set
  Facts
    1. To what is the speaker referring with the words, "Just follow him"?
    2. What conflict is expressed in this poem?
    3. What is being fought for in this poem?
  Issues
    1. On what occasions do we let others direct us? Why do we do this?
    2. When is it important for us to be in control?
    3. When is it harmful to let others control our lives?

An Unfailed Attempt

Facts

1. What does "not overspeaking my actions" look like?
2. What other actions are taken or not taken by the speaker?
3. How does the speaker contribute to his or her own dilemma and success?

Issues

1. When have your dilemmas been resolved to your satisfaction - but only as a result of a lengthy process?
2. How would our lives change if all problems were solved quickly?
3. In a society or one's family, who benefits when solutions are a lengthy process? Who benefits when they are expedient?

Courting Destiny

Facts

1. What is the nature of destiny that awaits the speaker?
2. What is the recommended way of courting destiny?
3. Explain the value placed on accomplishments.

Issues

1. Actions taken in a few moments of anger can destroy good works accomplished during a lifetime. Are there any other emotions that have such power?
2. Are there emotions and resulting actions that have the power to repair the destruction of an angry moment?
3. How do ministers and physicists differ in their advice for "courting destiny"?

Brothers

Facts

1. What is the focus of a "righteous brother"?
2. How could these ideas seem "too rational" or "too international"?
3. Why are national and international problems made so personal?

Issues

1. Are there national or international problems that could be resolved through individual commitment?

2. What barriers seem to prevent individual commitment to national/international solutions?
3. Sincerity, is a salient characteristic of this poem. How well do males and females fare when using sincerity? Is there a difference?

Always

Facts

1. This poem is meant to be a silly one, but what is the central idea?
2. What idea distinguishes each stanza?
3. If this poem were written as a piece of advice or a proverb, what would it be?

Issues

1. Why do new classes so often pose difficulties for us?
2. What are ways we can "keep loose" while facing new encounters?
3. What are the benefits of remaining open and accepting new experiences? What are the challenges?

Meet Me in NYC

Facts

1. Why do you think NYC is an attractive get-away for someone who'd love to visit Paris, Rome, or London?
2. How does one "paint the town up so pretty"?
3. What period of time does the character in this poem intend to stay in NYC - based on the message of the poem?

Issues

1. Why are cities regularly celebrated in songs or poetry?
2. What other cities are regularly celebrated by artists of all kinds?
3. What factors determine how timeless these celebrations become?

BEACONS OF lOVE

Misty

Facts

1. What is the setting where the scenes of stanzas one, two, and three are being carried out?
2. In the last line of the fourth stanza and the first line of the fifth stanza, what is meant by "play" and "playing"?
3. So, to whom or to what does the title "Misty" apply?

Issues

1. In a love affair, is the sum of the total greater than the whole - is the union of two individuals greater than the individuals independently acting on their own?
2. In a love affair, do we become more or less of who we really are?
3. If a relationship never goes beyond "frolicksomely light," is it a failed relationship?

Phoenix Friend

Facts

1. What is the myth of the phoenix that inspired this poem?
2. In what way does the character described reflect the phoenix?
3. How does one's soul "speak"?

Issues

1. This poem calls into question the idea of deja vu. What is your opinion of this type of experience?
2. The eyes are sometimes known as the mirrors of the soul. What can one's eyes express - even to strangers?
3. What quality in others allows us to feel "set free"?

Opposites

Facts

1. What is the message of this straight-forward poem?
2. What attitude does the speaker display? Which words or phrase/s support your assessment!
3. What is the attitude of the person who is the love interest of the speaker?

Issues

1. Is the ease with which this poem reads duplicated in the interactions of a relationship of opposites?
2. Dress and activities are a small part of a couple's interplay. As opposites, what additional areas of interaction would have a more significant impact on a couple's relationship?
3. Does the casual attitude of this speaker demonstrate respect or disinterest in the affairs of her love?

Pleasant Encounter

Facts

1. What 21st century attitudes are espoused in this poem?
2. What equity issues are taken for granted?
3. Which lines depict the self assuredness of a 21st century attitude?

Issues

1. Which activities, traditionally assigned to females, when adopted by a couple, appear to elevate the status of the female in the relationship?
2. Which activities, traditionally assigned to males, when adopted by a couple, appear to elevate the status of the male in a relationship?
3. In our modern times, how importatnt are gender specific roles and identities in a relationship?

Who's Chasing Whom

Facts

1. What are the speaker's ideas about what climate is necessary to encourage a relationship?
2. Why does the speaker now want to speak with such candor?
3. What reaction is the speaker expecting from this disclosure?

Issues

1. If successfully creating a relationship is like playing chess, why would there be disclosure about the moves before the game is over?
2. What are the plusses and minuses in using subtlety for pursuing any relationship?

3. What strengths are there in being direct in relationships?

Reality
Facts
1. Discuss which phrases lead to your opinion of whether this speaker's ideas are a reality or ironically, a phantom?
2. Explain the two very different views about life in the third stanza.
3. Is this a song to convince or to confirm? What words push you to your decision? What then is this speaker's new-found reality?

Issues
1. Is it possible to find "reality" in an individual?
2. Do older individuals or younger ones speak with such certainty? Why is this?
3. How does one define reality?

Passing Time
Facts
1. Are these the words of a gigolo, a floozy, a sincere person in love?
2. Passing time by sitting beside someone evening after evening can be incredibly boring. How does this "passing time" get its appeal?
3. What "one-line (cliche) pick-ups" can be culled from this song? How do they affect the sincerity of the speaker?

Issues
1. Songs create visions in our heads. Poems accomplish the same. What is the reason we keep coming back to the same visions in love songs and poems?
2. Peacefully, joyfully passing time together is a first step toward sealing "all ... tomorrows," but what are important next steps that are critical?
3. What are titles of other love songs that use repetition extensively?

Complete

Facts

1. How do you rectify the obvious dissonance created by "So complete your love is sweetness / I thought I was you" and "The time, the space I spent with you / I had forgot we'd shared"?
2. In your own words explain the idea of being complete as given by the poet.
3. Does the poet tip the scale making this a compliment rather than a critiical commentary?

Issues

1. What is your idea of feeling complete?
2. Then what conversely is the feeling of being incomplete?
3. Is the idea of being complete or incomplete an illusion created by young lovers?

Summer Madness

Facts

1. Explain the use of "summer" literally and figuratively.
2. Why does madness represent something as inspiring as love?
3. How does the setting match the mood of couples in love?

Issues

1. If in summer we have madness, what would a winter love be, or an autumn love, or a spring love?
2. Music is romantic. And therefore "your guitar ... and my songs" is appropriate imagery. What imagery would speak to the passion of love?
3. Describe one or two experiences with the madness that shows up whenever there is love.

No Recovery

Facts

1. What issues have caused this unhealable wound?
2. Will recovery ever be possible?
3. Is this a relationship worth saving?

Issues

1. It is *always* easier to recover from a failed affair when we end it. Why is recovery much more difficult when it is terminated by our love?

2. Is it altruistic or unhealthy to focus on a loved one's pain rather than our own when we are hurting?

3. Are we more or less realistic about affairs of the heart in our present twenty-first century times?

Write Me

Facts

1. What is the opening mood of this poem?

2. What is the situation of the speaker?

3. Does the mood of the poem change at the end of the lyrics?

Issues

1. Why does our society have the tendency to make this type of text gender specific? What gender would it be?

2. If the roles typically assigned to each gender were reversed, what would be your impression of the characters involved? Why?

3. How does our society benefit from identifying with role assignments by gender?

The Chill of Loneliness

Facts

1. What message is the speaker sending to her love?

2. Is there a message she also gives herself? What is that?

3. What do you think the speaker is inclined to do next, based on the hints given in the poem?

Issues

1. In our present times, do we communicate more or less with those we love? What facilitates more or fewer communications?

2. Comment on the state of a relationship that needs nightly calls?

3. Describe ways to inspire more frequent, healthy communications.

Going Fishing
Facts
1. What is the plot of this poem?
2. Cheating and making up is common. What attitude is evoked here by this cheating woman?
3. Replace every feminine pronoun with a masculine and visa versa. Are our attitudes different if it is a male who cheats?

Issues
1. America has always been infatuated with happy endings. Why is this?
2. Do happy endings prevent us from seeing reality, or does our focus on happy endings create our reality?
3. Does our society view women who cheat similarly or inequitably to men who cheat?

Ascension
Facts
1. What is the expectation of the speaker here?
2. Why will these events be of no surprise?
3. How many people are the focus of these lyrics. How many types of relationships do they share?

Issues
1. Why is success in relationships more likely when reached "with open eyes"?
2. How likely is it that two individuals can exhibit qualities that mirror those in relationships mentioned in stanza four?
3. Do contemporary relationships require fewer, or more, dimensions for their success than were necessary two or three generations ago?

Late Summer Storm
Facts
1. What is the literal storm to which the speaker refers?
2. What additional storm creates tension in this poem?
3. What is the resolution of both storms?

Issues
1. Does solace and comfort that eases one storm increase appreciation for another storm? What accounts for this?

2. In a relationship, describe a late summer storm?

3. Creature comforts have their place in easing any storm. In relationships, are creature comforts a solution or simply a setting for solutions to be worked out?

Confessions of the Accused
Facts
1. What anxieties plague the speaker's lovers?
2. Does this speaker's confession condemn or exonerate her?
3. As additional proof, who could additionally speak for the accused?

Issues
1. From your experiences with love, are there individuals who possess this capacity that the speaker describes?
2. Would there be a benefit for the speaker to alter her expressions of love? Or is there pleasure enough in sharing love that is deep and open?
3. "Time changes all things" is an old saying. Do you think it will also apply to this speaker's love?

Again
Facts
1. What is the irony of the encounters in "Again"?
2. Of these two distinct encounters, what remains the same?
3. What has changed?

Issues
1. Is there always a lag time between what our minds and hearts know? What accounts for this?
2. Does living make us tough-skinned or more sensitive and therefore responsive to our encounters?
3. Who, if anyone other than ourselves, might ever be aware of the changes that take place within us?

Returns to Puppy Love
Facts
1. What characterizes puppy love?
2. What is the benefit of memories of puppy love to this speaker?

3. For now, what is the state of the love life of the protagonist?

Issues

    1. Which love is more genuine: puppy love or that of a new day "balanced by the rain / And nurtured by the sun"?

    2. Are pleasant memories useful or a distraction to our learning and acceptance of what exists in our present?

    3. Is puppy love a pale comparison to intentional love, or is puppy love a necessary step toward intentional love?

NEMESIS? VANQUISH THEM.

Help Me ... For Now

Facts

    1. What irony is in the words of the speaker?

    2. What is his modus operandi?

    3. What face to the world does this speaker want to project?

Issues

    1. Is this a behavior that is more typical of men, women, or equally affected?

    2. How does this poem advocate for unconditional love?

    3. Is the behavior of the protagonist in the poem typical of human behavior? Does it therefore not need explanation nor apology?

The Boss/ Luxury

Facts

    1. What does the speaker say about naming things, and describing processes, and identifying the relationships? Why is it considered a luxury?

    2. Is this a source of contention for the speaker? Why

    3. Who are the fools, and what are their relationships to the boss?

Issues

    1. A certain amount of confidence comes with naming things, processes, and relationships. Is confidence a prerequisite for being boss or the result of being boss?

    2. Is carrying out the role of a boss a luxury or responsibility?

    3. What is the cost of this luxury that bosses have?

Competition's Complications

Facts

1. What is the speaker's complaint?
2. What does the poem suggest about gender construction in the U.S.?
3. What complication (and for whom) is described in the 6th stanza?

Issues

1. How does defining others dissipate their power as competitors?
2. Are the boxes that are prisons voluntary assignments that may be escaped at any time?
3. For those who are considered competitive targets, what are some useful ways to act in defiance?

Pseudo-Internation Dilettante

Facts

1. What elements characterize a "trans-world aura"?
2. "A hungry, hungry stare" suggests a hunger for what?
3. Why does the protagonist think those who dwell on thought of love are "so foolish"?

Issues

1. What are the arrogant conceits of a pseudo-international dilettante?
2. What are the ordinary standards by which we measure men?
3. What allows a pseudo-international dilettant to believe in his superior standards and thoughts?

Beyond Home

Facts

1. What is the dissatisfaction?
2. What is the attraction to that beyond home?
3. Explain to what it is that this journey leads? Is it a disappointment?

Issues

1. Routines may support us with a feeling of security or choke us with a feeling of loss for the spontaneously of life. With what oe with whom does the culpability lie?
2. Is it so that we are drawn to that which is similar or familiar?

Are there enough benefits beyond home to offset the difficulties
of our life-changing journeys?
3. Is the fiercest difficulty of a journey within the mind of a
traveler or without?

An American Horizon
Facts
1. How accurate is the description of an American horizon?
2. Describe the lives of those who live within this American
horizon?
3. What is the double-edged sword of the American horizon as
described in stanzas 2 and 4?
Issues
1. The same wealth may have a duplicitous affect. Is this a
dilemma that can be corrected? How?
2. What or who is typically unaccounted for in broad-stroke
visions of America?
3. Could there ever be a time that wealth would cause a flurry of
flight?

IN PRAISE OF ALL OUR MOMS
Thank You
Facts
1. What is most appreciated about this mother?
2. Besides thanking her mom, what additionally does this letter
attempt to do?
3. Explain "And today you peacefully sit, not asking for the world
- though mom, you gave it to us!"
Issues
1. When things go right, we thank our moms. When things go
wrong we blame our moms. How much of this thankfulness or
blame can be rightfully laid in the laps of our moms?
2. Is it true that cathected energy guides future relationships?
3. When, if ever, do we surface from this pool of cathected
energy?

Mother 12.98

Facts

1. What three comparisons are drawn to this mother?
2. How will the qualities live on?
3. What draw-back is inherent, though unmentioned, in each comparison?

Issues

1. Roses are not without thorns, love is not without it's conceits, the inertia of gold is not without its complications. So what balancing thorns, conceits, and complications are a part of being a mother?
2. Once a mother, always a mother. But when, if ever, does the relationship begin to shift and transform into other relationships?
3. Mothers pass on their strengths and challenges. But - as grandparents - do mothers so significantly change that their impact is more or less beneficial?

A Love Story

Facts

1. How does bravery factor into one's remaining stedfast?
2. What unspoken sacrifices are inherent in days filled with labor and nights filled with prayer?
3. Though mentioned only in the title and first stanza, what are this poet's understandings about love?

Issues

1. Some say the best way to learn is through the school of hard knocks. Some recommend virtual lessons? Which is likely to have the approval of the majority of society?
2. Though most mothers try their best to do well by their off spring, children, even in the same families, have varying degrees of appreciation for their moms. What factors come into play that make mothering - to the satisfaction of every child - such a difficult undertaking?
3. Love stories that seem to have the most currency are those that contain extreme challenges or end tragically? Why do we have a greater appreciation for love that hurts or wounds the protagonist?

Aunty 4.80
Facts

1. By the metaphorical language of the opening stanza, to what can our seasons of memory in song be additionally compared?
2. What additional comparison is implicit in this first stanza?
3. "With a song in my heart" and "... locked forever in my soul" convey the same message. What is that?

Issues

1. If your family songs are unpleasant, how do you erase or replace them?
2. What types of family songs are those which encourage and inspire us?
3. Each family has its song weaver, griot, or family storyteller. On what occasions does s/he tell them?

Aunty Emily
Facts

1. What are Aunty Emily's strengths?
2. What has she accomplished and is presently accomplishing with her young family members?
3. What are the gifts of exchange to Aunty Emily?

Issues

1. Is there an "Aunty Emily" in your family? What lessons has she passed on to you?
2. What type of enticements are most effective in encouraging young ones?
3. Even in communities where family members are fulfilling their respective roles, an "Aunty Emily" will surface. How are these Aunty Emily's in our own neighborhoods acknowledged? Could we do more?

Big Sis/Mother Earth
Facts

1. What qualities give Big Sis the sobriquet of Mother Earth?
2. Does Mother Earth attempt to spread her own advice or to pass on the advice of the multitudes to others?
3. What is the purpose of Mother Earth's climb?

Issues
1. What are the obvious drawbacks to a Mother Earth type?
2. What occupations would seem best suited to Mother Earth types?
3. What activities would be most confining and least enjoyable for Mother Earth?

Now I Lay Me Down to Sleep

Facts
1. What is the speaker's attitude toward those mentioned in this poem?
2. Who does this poem pray for?
3. What qualities does the speaker pray for?

Issues
1. What typical ways do we remember others in our prayers?
2. Many religions similarly honor their dead in addition to honoring those who are still alive. In what ways do we honor our dead in prayer?
3. What various religious practices and within what cultures and religions are the dead honored?

Tribute

Facts
1. What two distinct personalities are described as mothers?
2. How is time used by each of the mothers?
3. How does the child of each respond to its aging mom?

Issues
1. When does a mother know when her work is done?
2. Is sacrifice a requirement for parenting? Why?
3. Is it possible to repay a mother who has taken her role seriously and nurture a child successfully to adulthood?

We Gather 'Round You

Facts
1. In your own words, describe the mother who is spoken of in this poem?
2. What challenges are there for a child of this mother?

3. Is this mom considered a good mom?

Issues

    1. Is it possible for us to see our mothers with objectivity? When?

    2. Our opinions of our mothers change over time. Even if we are astute, are we ever or always accurate?

    3. Even for mothers who are unskilled in parenting, do we still "gather 'round"?

Our Mothers' Hearts

Facts

    1. What conflict and resolution is quickly disclosed?

    2. What hyperbolic comparisons revamp old cliches? What do they mean?

    3. What nationality does the phrase "turtle island rock" honor?

Issues

    1. We lean on our mothers for their wisdom and confidence. And in crisis, we find ourselves returning. When, if ever, do we stop returning to our mothers' presence for reassurance?

    2. If it is true that a mother-child connection is the hardest to sever, then why in a world of distrust and chaos do we not seek wisdom and strength of our mothers?

    3. If many women on their own face and accomplish such difficult tasks of raising children, who become the responsible adults of tomorrow, how is it that they are patronizingly referred to as "the weaker sex"?

THE FINISH GIVES MEANING TO THE RACE
A Mother's Desperation

Facts

    1. What encourages this mother to press on?

    2. Does hopefulness peek through this mother's prayer?

    3. Capricious as they may seem, how random are the touchstones used for encouragement by this mother?

Issues

    1. "The darkest hour is just before dawn." Explain your position as to whether or not this proverb applies to the speaker's attitude in this prayer?

2. How does the constancy of things – the ever-present skies, the countless and regular smiles of our children, the giggles and squeals of children everywhere – calm our jangled spirits enough to continue a challenging life?

3. Some things we cherish are considered small things. Why? Are they really?

Untouchable

Facts

1. How would this be restated from a mother to a small child?

Issues

1. In an age of sarcasm and "roasts" is there enough sincerity shown to our children?

Tomorrow's Painful Joy

Facts

1. What is this mother's vision for her son?

2. What observations does she make about her son in the present?

3. What is her emotion about her son's development into adulthood?

Issues

1. Explain the critical importance and influence of one's "work," one's chosen "path," and one's "love"?

2. Is it premature, obsessive, or responsible for mothers, while their children are still small enough to be lifted, to develop such concern about their children's futures.

3. Does a parent display altruism or selfishness by hurrying her child's future with such focus on it?

Lessons

Facts

1. What important lessons are implied?

2. What assumptions does this mother have about her son?

3. What is this mother's opinion about life's difficulties?

Issues

1. Explain the importance of light, rights, and dreams that are critical to quality of life?

2. Tell examples of childhood activities that taught intangible lessons?

3. Is this process of these lessons in reverse as powerful? Why? Why not?

Enigma

Facts

1. What is the speaker's opinion of this paradoxical young man?
2. What is this young man's currency in life?
3. What is the speaker's penchant for enigmas?

Issues

1. How does one become labelled an enigma??
2. How does stereotyping factor when dealing with enigmas?
3. When are each of us apt to remove the label of enigma from another person?

I Sit, II '01

Facts

1. In what activities is the speaker engaged?
2. Where is Danny presently?
3. What is the nature of the speaker's writing? Why is it so urgently written?

Issues

1. What is the quality of communication today when compared with the pre-computer technology era?
2. How has the emphasis changed over time as we communicate to others?
3. Timeless are messages and relationships. Are present-day communications strengthening these or disrupting their function?

Gentle

Facts

1. In what way does the need, acknowledged, also direct the reader?

Issues

1. In an era of high-tech speed, computer generated graphics, and explicit "in-your-face" exchanges, does one increase the effectiveness of communications using meiosis?

Somewhere There Is You

    Facts

        1. What is the conflict?

        2. How does the speaker's son improve her life?

        3. What must the speaker's son do?

    Issues

        1. Do most of our challenges originate within ourselves or outside of us?

        2. What popular practices througout the world do we use to eliminate stress or anxiety?

        3. Is the impact of inner tension imaginary or real? How do we know?

February Hugs .97

    Facts

        1. What is it that this mother is soliciting from her "village"?

        2. Why does the mother believe this is necessary?

        3. What would the age range of her son be for this to be effective?

    Issues

        1. How do parents determine the right doses of reality for their children?

        2. What does this poem communicate about messages that are unspoken?

        3. How do pets inform us about communications beyond the spoken word?

Forever Regulus

    Facts

        1. What qualities are touted by this poem?

        2. What unspoken appreciation is heralded by these elements as a collective?

        3. What quality then is celebrated in nature and in the young man to which this poem is directed?

    Issues

        1. How does this perspective fare in religious thought?

        2. How does this perspective fare with physics?

        3. How does this perspective fare with metaphysics?

All Pathways

Facts

1. Where do all pathways lead?
2. What is meant by, "... all pathways lead you home to God"?

Issues

1. What religious thought runs counter to the last line of this poem?
2. What religious thought supports the last line?
3. What does each belief reveal about the respective opinions (guiding principles) about human kind, and how is each belief manifested in the world?

A Continuum

Facts

1. What is the difference between knowledge and wisdom?

Issues

1. Is wisdom of less concern, admired less, more scarce, or simply being replaced by glamour and sophistication? What is the state of wisdom in the affairs of men and women today?

Danny's Music '98

Facts

1. When there are so many likes and dislikes in music, why does some music have universal appeal?
2. What are the virtues of music?
3. Explain the message in the fourth stanza?

Issues

1. Does success in one important area in our lives infatuate success in other areas as well? If so, how so?
2. What are other universal languages?
3. Why are widely acknowledged examples of universal language sometimes only acquired through premium prices; why are they so expensive?

Bless You

    Facts

        1. What are apparent interests for this son?

        2. Where does this son presently live?

        3. How is his age range established?

    Issues

        1. What does the image of flight imply?

        2. What are some of the uses of the term "flight" in day-to-day conversations?

        3. Why has this image retained such appeal throughout time?

On Turning 21

    Facts

        1. What is this mother acknowledging to her son?

        2. What have been some of this son's difficulties?

        3. What characteristics does this mother identify as facades?

    Issues

        1. Why do you think it is necessary for mothers to regularly and openly support tears that men shed?

        2. Why do you think boys are particularly susceptible to laboring long hours to obtain material things while it harms their quality of life?

        3. The limits that our society places around the expressions "real men" show may have a stultifying effect. Why are limits placed? What is the effect to themselves and others?

Educator's Guide: Poetry Exploration and Essay Suggestions

Guide

GIVE THE FATHERLESS BOY SOME ELBOW ROOM

I'll Tell You A Story ...

    Strategies

        1. What mood/s are projected in this poem?

        2. Which words or phrases help to signal the moods?

        3. Of the many layers of poetry (figurative language, rhyme, rhythm, innovations in conventions) which is most striking? Give an example and explain.

Bounce

    Strategies

        1. Is this poem dramatic, lyric, or a ballad? Why?

        2. How does the title of the poem reflect the poem? How does it reflect contemporary language of the 21st century?

        3. Explain the use of sunlight, night, and shadow?

You Are Not Your Father

    Strategies

        1. How does mention of Santa, the Easter Bunny, the Tooth Fairy, and the Sand Man impact the message of this poem?

        2. What is the significance of using hyperbole in this poem? Identify examples and explain the importance of each instance.

        3. Identify the ways which the poet indicates are possibilities in one's life.

Never Let them Tell You Who You Are

    Strategies

        1. At one point, the pace of this poem quickens. When does this happen, and how does this affect the poem?

        2. How do the personal details of the character addressed make you feel about that person? Why did the poet make a point of including these?

3. What point could be made by the use of the ellipses at the end of the poem?

The Universe Whispers Weapons
   Strategies
      1. To what mother does this black child's mother defer?
      2. How does love, humility, boldness, and an ability to hear whispers make a warrior more likely to win his battles?
      3. What makes nature irreverently, relentlessly truthful?

Topics for Writing
      1. What options would unlock to everyone if men felt free from castigation for openly expressing themselves? Write about what changes you believe would result if behaviors weren't genderized.
      2. In 3 columns list the behaviors acceptable for women, the behaviors acceptable for "gay men," and the behaviors acceptable for "real men." How is it that the options for "real men" are so narrow, and those for women and "gay men" are so plentiful? Discuss the reasons as you see them..
      3. War - the ultimate solution? What if war were not viewed as an option - but as a failure? Write a paper detailing steps, presently avoided, that could become a matter of record in a new or amended system for nations to resolve differences?

OUR VIGILANTLY INDEPENDENT SONS
Two Generations At Breakfast
   Strategies
      1. How does the use of hyperbole contribute to our understanding of the four characters?
      2. What mood is generated in the fourth stanza? Which words in particular contribute to this mood?
      3. The poet uses periods sparsely. How does this affect the sense of timing for the events in the poem?

The Lake

Strategies

1. Of the poetic layers (rhyme, rhythm, figurative language, innovations in conventions), which contributes most to the mood of the character?
2. Which layer contributes most to the tone of the poem?
3. The second stanza reads, "No one is here to hear me / If I should cry before I wake / From this bad dream without my love / No one's here but my friend the lake." This is an allusion to the words from a child's prayer, "Now I lay me down to sleep. ..." What effect does this allusion have on your understanding of the poem?

Train

Strategies

1. How does repetition and rhythm tie into the title, "Train?"
2. At the closing of this poem, What is the resolution?
3. Can this train be literal? Figurative? Both? Why?

Prehension

Strategies

1. How does the staggered position every other line in the text affect the message of the poem?
2. As you scan the text, identify the rhythm.
3. What poetic device demonstrates the empowerment of the poem's character?

Perennial Weather

Strategies

1. Identify the feet and meter.
2. With the poetic license of creating a new word - "couplement," what dimension is brought to the poem?
3. How would the flow of the poem be affected if "couplement" were changed to a conventional word?

Past Remembered
  Strategies
    1. Take the symbols of "melody" and "symphony." What type of behavior or interaction is suggested by each?
    2. Explain the metaphor of "riddled through the ocean waves ...."
    3. How does the repetition of the second stanza contribute to the poem?

Transparent Lures
  Strategies
    1. What mood is created by the imagery expressed here?
    2. As synecdoches, what do the eyes, mouths, and hands in this poem represent?
    3. What is meant by "mutable stone"?

Nectar in a Sieve
  Strategies
    1. What does this title tell us about the poem?
    2. Is the title a statement of the action or the result of the poem?
    3. Like childhood, why could nectar lose its appeal?

A New Face on the Set
  Strategies
    1. What metaphors are used?
    2. To what do these metaphors refer?
    3. From the lines of this poem, as a picture, what is the setting?

An Unfailed Attempt
  Strategies
    1. How do you believe an "Unfailed Attempt" would be different than a "Successful Attempt"?
    2. To what does "currency" refer when attempting to transpose or decode?
    3. What is the setting of this poem? How does it contribute to the conflict and eventually to the resolution?

Courting Destiny

Strategies

1. Why would this be considered a dramatic poem?
2. What effect is given by the transition from 1st person plural at the opening of the poem, to 1st person singular at the end?
3. Is this poem offered as a recommendation or an affirmation?

Brothers

Strategies

1. For many reasons, this message is inconsistent with contemporary, trendy, poetic style. What are the most salient inconsistencies?
2. What currency does the sincerity of this poem have in today's world?
3. Transpose one stanza into poetic rap. How is the message impacted?

Always

Strategies

1. What words contribute heavily to the mood?
2. Understanding innovations of grammar contribute to our understanding of this poem. Rewrite each sentence with corrected syntax.
3. The difficulty of writing such a poem is created by the alphabetized vocabulary. Try one.

Meet Me in NYC

Strategies

1. Is the style of this poem that of a narrative, a dramatic poem, or lyrics of a song? What qualities help you decide?
2. Although not written, how does the character in this poem hint about the attributes of NYC?
3. This poem depicts thoughts of a working-class person. What words or phrase specifically hits the demographic of the character speaking?

Topics for Writing

1. What laws would not be necessary if societies encouraged men and women to follow their dreams regardless to whether they fit the socially correct gender associations? Examine and discuss the benefits that would result and the labels that would lose their currency.?

2. What brilliant leaders might surface in our culturally diverse world if we directed our attention to the solution of issues rather than minimizing diversity? Describe when you misjudged someone whose solution, if heard, would have positively affected a high stake outcome.

3. What struggles, ineqities, and unfair advantages would be lost if ideas for the good of all were more highly valued and deliberated than taking sides for the sake of increasing a commonly acknowledged group's power? Select 2 opposing, culturally charged perspectives from members of 2 different cultural populations. - not your own. Detail each perspective. Attempt to create a compromise where both feel honored. Then write of the difficulties involved.

BEACONS OF LOVE

Misty

Strategies

1. In what way/s does the poet depict the confusion or identify the organization that typifies this affair?
2. How does the poet's character describe "heavy heat"?
3. How does the poet depict her neutrality in judging the two personalities?

Phoenix Friend

Strategies

1. With the focus of this poem being only on a face, eyes, and one's heart, what does each represent?
2. Such natural elements as fire and water come into play in this poem. What does each represent?
3. What dimension does repetition bring to this poem?

Opposites

Strategies

    1. Although this poem is written about opposites, on whom or in what does this poem actually focus?

    2. Poems that are used for lyrics may contain repetition that becomes a bridge. What could be used as a bridge in this poem?

    3. If the title of this poem were based on the attitude of the speaker, what would be the title?

Pleasant Encounter

Strategies

    1. The association of a gender to specific images is consistent with traditional thought, what are the phrases that contain these images?

    2. Has the poet moved the speaker's actions in the poem toward or away from a particular gender identity? Are there phrases that belie this movement?

    3. As a dramatic poem, how does the voice extend the speaker's assertiveness? How would a third person perspective affect the feeling of assertiveness that the speaker delivers?

Who's Chasing Whom

Strategies

    1. What irony is described?

    2. What is the obvious bridge for this poem or set of lyrics?

    3. From examining the words of the speaker, describe the speaker's effectiveness with subtlety in her disclosure and in her pursuit of her love.

Reality

Strategies

    1. What impact do these words "one truth," "forever," "eternally" have on this speaker's credibility?

    2. These lyrics contain hyperbole. What does hyperbole contribute to the lyrics of a song?

    3. If this were an essay, what impact would hyperbole have?

Passing Time
Strategies
    1. Songs of all sorts traditionally use much repetition. Why is repetition popular?

    2. What can be beguiling is what is not said. What is not said, in this poem, but could be said in our contemporary age?

    3. Has this convention of subtlety lost its popularity?

Complete
Strategies
    1. A critical commentary or a compliment? How is this accomplished?

    2. Does the idea of completeness fit in the same category, or act as an oppositional balance to the metaphorical statements and hyperbole in these lyrics?

    3. How does this compact set of lyrics exemplify "completeness"?

Summer Madness
Strategies
    1. What accounts for the light-hearted attitude of these lyrics?

    2. What sayings, passed for generations, contribute to the image of rain represented by tears?

    3. In summer we typically focus on the foliage in bloom. Is the setting of the summer sky more appropriate for "Summer Madness"?

No Recovery
Strategies
    1. What irony is woven into the text of this poem?

    2. What images place us into the proper era of this poem?

    3. What words or phases speak to the passion and trauma of this poem?

Write Me

Strategies

1. These lyrics involve a simple plot. What elements are present?
2. How is the mood established?
3. How does the poet keep these lyrics from falling into a depressing plea?

The Chill of Loneliness

Strategies

1. What does the poet say is the chill of loneliness?
2. How is passion made visible in this poem?
3. How does the poet maintain a lightness to this poem so that it doesn't become sad and wanting pity?

Going Fishing

Strategies

1. Bending or breaking rules of grammar is common in poetry and lyrics. How does this impact the poem?
2. Comparing fishing to finding new love has a history. Why is this such a long standing comparison? Why does it work?
3. Other elements of nature are also images in these lyrics. What dimensions does nature provide that more contemporary or man-made images cannot?

Ascension

Strategies

1. What is implied about this relationship, by the title, "Ascension"?
2. What is the purpose of the image created by the sultry stream?
3. What is the purpose of the contrasts in the fourth stanza?

Late Summer Storm

Strategies

1. How is tension created and assuaged within this setting?
2. How do the primary and secondary events enhance one another?

3. How does the title of this poem forecast the amicability of protagonists at the end of the poem?

Confessions of the Accused
Strategies
1. How does the poet characterize the speaker's personality?
2. What, about the speaker, seems to have frightened her loves?
3. What about the accused's conversation leads you to believe that she will never change?

Again
Strategies
1. How does parallelism affect the message of this poem?
2. How is irony achieved?
3. What imagery explains the changes in the protagonist?

Returns to Puppy Love
Strategies
1. What ideas are conjured by images of puppies?
2. Symbolic are the clothesline, sun, and rain. What does each stand for?
3. What would this protagonist say of extremes and of balance?

Topics for Writing
1. Can we learn about our treatment of others through our awarenesses when we experience love? Examine and discuss the changes in attitude and behavior of someone in love. Which changes would be welcomed if permanently exhibited?
2. Some of the greatest love songs are written by men? Explore one. What does it tell us about the depth of men's emotions that are sometimes cloaked in machismo?
3. Many love songs are performed by men. Who are some examples? What is our attraction to songs performed by such men as Luther Van Dross, Perry Como, Baby Face?

NEMESIS? VANQUISH THEM

Help Me ... For Now

Strategies

1. What does the hyperbole tell you about the speaker's self-image?
2. How does the poet display this character's lack of sensitivity?
3. What is meant by not forgetting "...where / You laid down your / Walking shoes"?

The Boss' Luxury

Strategies

1. What key words or phrases help to create the mood?
2. How does the poet establish the subjectivity of the boss' declarations?
3. What is the implication of stanza 2 and 3 for the speaker?

Competition's Complications

Strategies

1. How is the assault on the speaker's character achieved?
2. How does the speaker create ridicule?
3. Whose side is the poet on? How do you know?

Pseudo-International Dilettante

Strategies

1. What phrases reveal the poet's attitude toward the protagonist?
2. By what method does the poet disclose these attitudes?
3. In what way does the poet turn us away from siding with the protagonist?

Beyond Home

Strategies

1. What method ties the reader to a first-hand experience of this journey?
2. How does the nature of the journey compare to the journey's end? What is the effect?
3. How does the journey's end compare to the opening dissatisfaction?

An American Horizon
 Strategies
  1. What view does the poet take by using an ant metaphor?
  2. How is the speaker's change of perspective signalled?
  3. What signals a change in the tone of the speaker as the
   poem progresses?

Topics for Writing
  1. Describe a personality characteristic that matches our
   society's gender stereotype. Explain why it is necessarily
   assigned to this gender? Or is it necessary?
  2. Describe what you have seen in movies about war. Interview
   someone who has served in the front lines of war. Tell how
   these two differ.
  3. When public pressure to conform clashes with our strongly felt
   needs, what options do we have for allaying the pressure? List
   your suggestions for upholding and advancing your
   perspective on one such issue..

IN PRAISE OF ALL OUR MOMS
Thank You
 Strategies
  1. What is accomplished by presenting this poem as a letter and
   leaving it unsigned?
  2. Why, in such a personal letter, does the poet speak in first
   person plural?
  3. What benefits are there in the contrasts within this letter?

Mother 12 '98
 Strategies
  1. Sensuality, passion, and faith are not necessary qualities for
   mothers to possess. How does the poet limit the extent of
   influence of this poem?
  2. What would be the effect if the ideas presented in the last
   stanza were presented first?
  3. How does the poet develop rising expectation for the
   climax?

A Love Story
>Strategies
>>1. How is this poem atypical of a love story?
>>2. What feeling is intentionally evoked by the last single-word stanza?
>>3. What evidence presented here would argue that this is a mother on her own?

Aunty 4 '80
>Strategies
>>1. The tenor of these songs convey what type of history is being retold?
>>2. Family stories have varying degrees of usefulness. How would these family stories be helpful?
>>3. Who is obviously the weaver of songs in this family?

Aunty Emily
>Strategies
>>1. There are consistent feet and meters in this poem. Identify them?
>>2. What energy and urgency dominates this poem through the rhythm?
>>3. How is the age and wisdom of Aunty Emily easily rendered?

Big Sis/Mother Earth
>Strategies
>>1. Are there limits to Mother Earth's understanding? Why?
>>2. Why does Mother Earth flourish from drinking and talking with others?
>>3. Is Mother Earth's role that of expansion or maintenance?

Now I Lay Me Down to Sleep
>Strategies
>>1. What allusion dominates this poem?
>>2. How does the poet convey the speaker's regard for those she mentions?
>>3. How does the speaker express her shortcomings?

Tribute
  Strategies
    1. How does the poet manipulate cliches to increase their effect in the third stanza?
    2. What other cliches are used? How do they impact the message of the poet?
    3. What is the effect of the speaker discussing her mom at the opening and closing of this poem?

We Gather 'Round You
  Strategies
    1. If the poet displays objectivity, how is it achieved?
    2. How does the brevity of each stanza support the metaphor?
    3. What do the metaphors of flame, rain, leaves, and light stand for?

Our Mothers' Hearts
  Strategies
    1. How does the fantasy of the second stanza mark the deference given mothers?
    2. How does the movement of first person plural to the ending apostrophe serve the message of this poem?
    3. Elaborate on the title of this poem as a synecdoche.

Topics for Writing
    1. Write about the behaviors and unhealthy ties that exist for a "Mama's Boy." Tell how this extreme cripples both mother and son.
    2. Examine the life of a famous son who has been raised by his mom. Compare their struggles and resulting strengths to one raised by both parents. Explain what accounts for the differences.
    3. Describe the charities and influence of a community mom?

THE FINISH GIVES MEANING TO THE RACE

A Mother's Desperation
    Strategies
        1. How does the poet display a quiet hopefulness?
        2. How constant are the objects of focus for this mother?
        3. How does this prayer speak to the strength of this mother?

Untouchable
    Strategies
        1. Explain the use of metonymy and synecdoche?

Tomorrow's Painful Joy
    Strategies
        1. What figure of speech is the title of this poem, and how do you explain it's use?
        2. How does the poem achieve its emotion and tone?
        3. What areas of her child's life do synecdoches establish as the mother's focus?

Lessons
    Strategies
        1. Does this speaker have her own perspective that she wishes to convey to her child?
        2. By what method does this mother expect her child to learn?
        3. What relationship does this speaker believe exists between tangible and intangible? About processes?

Enigma
    Strategies
        1. How is this poem kept from becoming a "grocery list" of attributes?
        2. Where is the movement that floats this poem?
        3. What is the impact of the poet's use of apostophe?

I Sit, 11'01
    Strategies
        1. How do we come to understand the speaker's meaning of "listening and planning"?

2. In what stanza/s does the speaker convey her dissatisfactions? And they are ... ?
3. In what way is this poem tied to contemporary times?

Gentle
Strategies
1. Speak to the use of synecdoche? Does the brevity and subtlety also indicate the use of meiosis?

Somewhere There Is You
Strategies
1. What message is conveyed by the water image?
2. How is it carried through this poem?
3. Where does the tension occur for the speaker? How do the stanzas work to enhance tension?

February Hugs '97
Strategies
1. What elements of this poem mirror those in an essay?
2. What qualities help this remain poetry?
3. How does the format of this poem encourage understanding and help to clarify the message?

Forever Regulus
Strategies
1. What is the poet's intent with these comparisons to the grass, wind, sun, ocean, skies, stars?
2. What two nationalities are evoked by use of the last stanza?
3. Is the movement of this poem from specific to general or vice versa? What is the effect?

All Pathways
Strategies
1. Explain the metaphor of "God's Light at your feet to wisdom leads."

A Continuum
Strategies
1. What traditional belief is carried by the poet's message?

Danny's Music '98
Strategies
1. How does the layout of the poem affect the content?
2. What is the intent of the fourth stanza? And the poem?
3. The intent of the poem is disclosed in the latter half of the poem. What is the reason for the first half?

Bless You
Strategies
1. Is this poem to be directed to her son, or in the style of a prayer?
2. So for whose benefit was this poem written?
3. How does this poem reveal a closeness between the mother and son?

On Turning 21
Strategies
1. How does this mother express her acceptance of all religious orders?
2. How does the speaker demonstrate equity for each gender?
3. What messages are tied to the metonymys used in the fourteenth and fifteenth stanzas?

Topics for Writing
1. What legacies will be left by famous men raised by their moms? Examine the life of a neighborhood hero. What part of his achievement is identifiably the result of his mother's caregiving or teachings? Ask him.
2. Examine the life of a famous man raised by both parents. What part of his achievement was shaped by his mother's caregiving and advice?

3. Interview a young adult or mature man about his mother, whether he was raised by a mother on her own or both parents. What are his thoughts about his mother's care, advice, interactions, negotiations, visions for him? What additionally was the impact of those interactions with his father? What new awareness did you gain?

CPSIA information can be obtained at www.ICGtesting.com
Printed in the USA
BVOW07s0526190813

328868BV00003B/353/A